This Journal Belongs To

_____

My intention for this sacred journey:

_____

_____

_____

"I open this journal as a sacred vessel for truth
and transformation. I welcome the language of my
dreams as divine guidance.
I walk this path with devotion, trust, and love."

Journey Guide

Journey Guide

To the Dreamer

A Poetic Invitation to Your Journey

This journal is a **sacred companion**, designed to guide you through the landscape of your dreams and intuition. Explore the depths of your inner world, where every page invites reflection and inspiration. With soft gold accents and serene imagery, may this journal nurture your spirit and illuminate your path towards transformation and divine awakening.

This journal is dedicated to you—

The dreamer who listens to the quiet spaces between breath and heartbeat.

The seeker who trusts the unseen, and finds meaning in moonlight and silence.

The soul who has walked through shadows only to discover that light was within all along.

May these pages hold your whispers, your revelations, your rebirths.

May each symbol become a teacher, each reflection a prayer.

And may your nights become sacred journeys that awaken your days.

"You are the dream and the dreamer.
You are the question and the answer.
You are the light remembering itself."

Sacred Introduction – The Language of Dreams

Before the first light of day, your soul speaks in symbols. Each dream is a whisper
from the divine, a poem written in the language of your own becoming.

This journal is not merely a place to record those whispers—
it is a vessel for transformation, a sacred space where the unseen
becomes seen.

Dreams are messengers of truth.

They rise from the deep waters of your intuition, carrying the
essence of healing, revelation, and guidance. This is a devotional
practice of remembering who you are:
divine presence in human form.

Invocation:
*"May these pages become a mirror for the sacred within.
May each dream guide me back to truth,
And may I walk this path with grace, wonder, and devotion."*

Sacred Introduction –
The Language of Dreams

How to Use This Journal – A Sacred Practice
Before you begin, remember that this is not a journal to be filled—
it is a sanctuary to be entered.

Create Your Space:
Light a candle or breathe deeply to center yourself.
Let silence soften the mind. Record Your Dreams Upon Waking:
Write freely, before logic filters the message.
Note emotions, colors, and sensations.

Work with the Moon:
Set intentions under the New Moon and reflect under the Full Moon.
Let lunar cycles rhythm your journey.

Listen to the Subtle:
Sometimes meaning comes not in words but in feeling.
Trust the quiet wisdom that arises as you write.

Sacred Reminder:
"You are not analyzing your dreams—you are conversing with your soul."

The Ancient Tree- Roots of Wisdom and Growth

Strength comes from remembering where you come from. You are supported by generations of wisdom and love.

Affirmation

"I grow strong and steady. My roots are deep, my spirit limitless."

Breath Ritual

Inhale as if drawing strength from the roots below.
Exhale tension into the soil.

Dream Summary

You find yourself beneath a massive ancient tree. Its roots stretch deep into the earth while branches reach toward the stars.

Symbolic Meaning

Tree: Stability, ancestral wisdom, and the bridge between earth and sky.

Roots: Foundation, heritage, grounding.

Branches: Expansion, reaching toward dreams and growth.

Dream Log

Emotion, Message, Insight for each dream

Journal Prompts

What roots nourish my growth?
How can I balance being grounded and reaching higher?
Which traditions or memories strengthen me?

The Mountain Path - Journey of Strength and Ascent

Every step of the climb has shaped your resilience. Rest in the knowing that progress itself is sacred.

Breath Ritual

Inhale courage.
Exhale gratitude for the journey

Symbolic Meaning

Mountain: Strength, perseverance, and higher perspective.

Climb: The effort of spiritual or personal growth.

Summit: Clarity after challenge.

Affirmation

"I am steady and strong. Each step brings me closer to clarity."

Dream Summary

You climb a tall mountain, the air crisp and clear. At the summit, you feel an overwhelming sense of peace.

Dream Log

Emotion, Message, Insight for each dream

Journal Prompts

What challenges am I rising above?
How do I find peace in the process, not just the goal?
What have I already conquered that I can honor now?

The Warm Home – Sanctuary of Belonging and Safety

You are creating a sanctuary within yourself. Each part of you deserves warmth and acceptance.

Affirmation

"I am at home within myself. I welcome every part of my being."

Breath Ritual

Inhale as if drawing strength from the roots below.
Exhale tension into the soil.

Dream Summary

You wander through a home that feels both familiar and new. Each room glows with golden light.

Symbolic Meaning

Home: The psyche's reflection of inner safety.

Rooms: Aspects of self or life areas being illuminated.

Light: Awareness and healing of emotional spaces.

Dream Log

Emotion, Message, Insight for each dream

Journal Prompts

Which parts of myself feel like home?
Are there inner rooms I avoid visiting?
What does true emotional safety mean to me?

The Soaring Birds – Messengers of Spirit and Freedom

Your soul is calling you to rise above distraction and trust your intuition. A new perspective will reveal your next step.

Affirmation

"I trust my inner wings. My vision expands with clarity and grace."

Symbolic Meaning

Birds: Freedom, perspective, connection to higher guidance.

Flight: Rising above old patterns and limits.

Single Bird: Focused intuition; your higher self seeking your attention.

Breath Ritual

Inhale deeply through the nose, lifting the heart.
Exhale slowly, releasing limitation.
Repeat until your mind feels light.

Dream Summary

Your soul is calling you to rise above distraction and trust your intuition. A new perspective will reveal your next step.

Dream Log

Emotion, Message, Insight for each dream

Journal Prompts

Where am I being asked to take flight in life?
What thoughts or habits weigh me down?
What message do I feel my intuition is trying to deliver?

The Living Soil – Foundation of Growth and Nourishment

What feels heavy or broken may actually be compost for your growth. Transformation starts below the surface.

Affirmation

"I am nourished by every experience. I grow in the richness of life."

Breath Ritual

Exhale stress into the ground. Inhale strength from the earth.

Dream Summary

You dig your hands into rich, dark soil. Worms and roots pulse with life energy beneath your fingertips.

Symbolic Meaning

Soil: Nourishment, fertility, transformation through decay.

Touching Earth: Reconnection with nature's cycles.

Life Beneath: Hidden energy, rebirth through grounding.

Dream Log

Emotion, Message, Insight for each dream

Journal Prompts

What old experiences are feeding my current growth?
How can I reconnect with the natural world to ground my
energy?
What part of me is ready to bloom?

The Mirror Reflection – Truth of Self and Perception

You are evolving into a clearer version of yourself. Trust what is being revealed—not everything that changes is loss.

Affirmation

"I see myself clearly and lovingly. Awareness brings liberation."

Symbolic Meaning

Mirror: Self-awareness, reflection, seeing truth.

Changing Faces: Shifting identities, layers of the self.

Calm Reflection: Clarity after confusion; self-acceptance.

Breath Ritual

Inhale: "Awareness."
Exhale: "Acceptance."
Repeat three times while focusing on your heart center.

Dream Summary

You stand before a mirror. At first, your reflection shifts and changes, showing different versions of you before settling into a calm, radiant image.

Dream Log

Emotion, Message, Insight for each dream

Journal Prompts

How do I perceive myself when I'm most aligned?
What reflections (from others or situations) are
teaching me right now?
What am I ready to see clearly without judgment?

The Sunrise Horizon – Awakening of Hope and Possibility

A new chapter is dawning. The clarity you seek is rising from within—trust the light emerging in your life.

Affirmation

"Each dawn brings new wisdom. I awaken with purpose and grace."

Breath Ritual

Inhale light through the crown. Exhale warmth into the heart. Visualize the sun within you expanding.

Dream Summary

You watch the sun rise over a quiet landscape. The light spills across the world, illuminating hidden colors and forms.

Symbolic Meaning

Sunrise: Renewal, new awareness, inspiration.

Light Emerging: Clarity after confusion; awakening energy.

Horizon: Infinite potential, forward vision.

Dream Log

Emotion, Message, Insight for each dream

Journal Prompts

What new awareness is rising in me now?
What morning practices help me feel aligned?
How can I begin each day with curiosity instead of pressure?

The Waterfall – Cleansing Flow of Emotion and Power

Let emotions move freely. Surrender control and allow intuition to wash away resistance.

Affirmation

"I flow effortlessly with life. Clarity comes through surrender."

Symbolic Meaning

Waterfall: Flow of emotion, cleansing, intuitive renewal.

Mist & Light: Healing through release; clarity through surrender.

Standing Before It: Readiness to embrace your emotional flow.

Breath Ritual

Inhale through the nose, exhale with a sigh. Imagine energy flowing like water through your body.

Dream Summary

You stand before a cascading waterfall. Mist covers your face as sunlight dances through the spray. You feel renewed and alive.

Dream Log

Emotion, Message, Insight for each dream

Journal Prompts

Where in my life can I let go and trust the flow?
What emotions are seeking expression right now?
How do I feel when I release instead of control?

The All-Seeing Eyes – Cleansing Flow of Emotion and Power

The truth you seek is already within you. You are being guided to trust your inner knowing and look deeper.

Affirmation

"I see with both my heart and intuition. Truth illuminates my path."

Breath Ritual

Close your eyes, breathe slowly. On each inhale, whisper: "I see."
On each exhale, whisper: "I trust."

Dream Summary

You feel the gaze of unseen eyes in a dream—not judgmental, but knowing.
Then you realize they are your own eyes, wide open in awareness.

Symbolic Meaning

Eyes: Perception, intuition, and spiritual awakening.

Seeing Yourself: Integration of inner and outer sight.

Unseen Presence: Trusting the unseen; awakening higher perception.

Dream Log

Emotion, Message, Insight for each dream

Journal Prompts

What am I finally ready to see clearly?
When have I ignored my intuition, and what did I learn?
How can I honor my inner vision daily?

The Golden Key – Unlocking Potential and Divine Access

You hold the power to unlock your own path. The opportunity you seek is already within reach—trust your readiness.

Affirmation

"The key to my success is within me. I unlock doors through clarity and confidence."

Symbolic Meaning

Key: Unlocking potential, empowerment, opportunity.

Gold: Divine timing and value; inner treasures revealed.

Holding the Key: Realization that you already possess what's needed.

Breath Ritual

Inhale: "Open."
Exhale: "Receive."
Repeat three times, visualizing a door of golden light opening before you.

Dream Summary

You discover a glowing golden key in your hand. It feels warm, as though alive. A sense of anticipation fills you as you wonder what it will open.

Dream Log Template

Emotion, Message, Insight for each dream

Journal Prompts

What new possibility is waiting for me to open the door?
What do I already have that I may be overlooking?
How can I align my intention with inspired action?

The Doorway -Threshold of Becoming

You are on the threshold of transformation. Courage is the key to stepping through uncertainty into manifestation.

Affirmation

"I walk through doors of opportunity with trust and courage."

Breath Ritual

Visualize inhaling golden light as the door opens.
Exhale gently and step through in your mind's eye.

Dream Summary

You stand before a door—sometimes ancient, sometimes modern. You hesitate before opening it, unsure what lies beyond.

Symbolic Meaning

Door: Transition, choice, or opportunity.

Closed Door: Resistance, timing, or preparation.

Opening It: Stepping into new purpose with courage.

Dream Log

Emotion, Message, Insight for each dream

Journal Prompts

What threshold am I standing before in my life or work?
What fears make me hesitate to open the next door?
How can I honor my intuition as I step forward?

The Fire Within – Flame of Passion and Transformation

Your creative energy is awakening. Let passion guide you but remember—controlled fire sustains, uncontrolled fire consumes.

Affirmation

"My inner fire fuels my purpose. I create with clarity and joy."

Symbolic Meaning

Fire: Creative passion, transformation, vitality.

Flame: Focused willpower and direction.

Warmth: Empowerment without burnout.

Breath Ritual

Inhale through the nose, hold for a moment of heat in the solar plexus, exhale slowly. Repeat while visualizing a steady golden flame.

Dream Summary

You see a campfire or inner flame burning brightly. It doesn't harm but fills you with strength and motivation.

Dream Log Template

Emotion, Message, Insight for each dream

Journal Prompts

What passion or idea is ready to ignite?
How can I channel my energy productively?
What boundaries help me maintain steady
creative flow?

The Bridge Crossing – Passage Between Worlds

You are bridging the gap between vision and reality. Each small step you take aligns your inner and outer worlds.

Affirmation

"I bridge vision and action with trust. Each step is progress."

Breath Ritual

Inhale: "Align." Exhale: "Flow."
Imagine walking confidently across your inner bridge.

Dream Summary

You approach a bridge spanning a river or canyon. As you cross, you sense a shift—what lies on the other side feels lighter and clearer.

Symbolic Meaning

Bridge: Connection, transition, integration.

Crossing: Moving from intention to realization.

River Below: Flow of time and emotion.

Dream Log Template

Emotion, Message, Insight for each dream

Journal Prompts

What am I transitioning toward right now?
How can I connect my dreams to consistent action?
What support helps me stay steady as I cross my next
bridge?

The Flowing River – Current of Life and Letting Go

The flow of life is carrying you exactly where you're meant to go. Let go of the need to control the direction—trust the current.

Affirmation

"I am in the flow of divine timing. I move with ease toward my goals."

Symbolic Meaning

River: Purpose in motion, surrender, divine timing.

Changing Currents: Life's adaptability and natural rhythm.

Following It: Trust in unfolding journey.

Breath Ritual

Inhale deeply through the nose, exhale with a gentle wave sound. Visualize the current carrying you forward with grace.

Dream Summary

You follow a river through ever-changing landscapes—sometimes calm, sometimes wild—yet it always leads you forward.

Dream Log

Emotion, Message, Insight for each dream

Journal Prompts

Where am I resisting the natural flow of events?
What would it feel like to trust my process fully?
How can I align my work with life's rhythm instead of force?

The Butterfly Emergence – Metamorphosis of the Soul

You have outgrown old limitations. Trust the beauty of becoming—transformation is both delicate and powerful.

Affirmation

"I am evolving into my true form. I honor every stage of my transformation."

Breath Ritual

Inhale expansion. Exhale release.
Visualize wings unfolding as you breathe.

Dream Summary

You watch a butterfly emerge from its cocoon, fragile yet radiant. It flutters uncertainly, then finds its rhythm in the air.

Symbolic Meaning

Butterfly: Transformation, personal growth, freedom.

Cocoon: Period of healing and preparation.

Emergence: Rebirth and embracing a new self.

Dream Log

Emotion, Message, Insight for each dream

Journal Prompts

What part of my life is ready to transform?
What stage of metamorphosis am I currently in—cocoon,
emergence, or flight?
How can I honor my growth process with patience?

The Phoenix Rising – Rebirth from Ashes to Light

Let go of what no longer serves. From release comes renewal—your new life is being born from the ashes of the old.

Affirmation

"I am reborn through transformation. Every ending fuels my renewal."

Symbolic Meaning

Phoenix: Renewal, rebirth, strength after endings.

Fire: Purification and courage to let go.

Ashes: The fertile ground of new beginnings.

Breath Ritual

Inhale deeply, feeling warmth in your chest.
Exhale fully, releasing the old energy into light.

Dream Summary

A great bird of flame bursts into ashes before being reborn, glowing brighter than before. You feel renewed energy radiating through you.

Dream Log

Emotion, Message, Insight for each dream

Journal Prompts

What is burning away to make room for rebirth?
What am I learning from the endings in my life?
What version of myself is ready to rise?

The Cleansing Storm – Growth Through Beauty and Devotion

Healing often comes through feeling. Let your emotions wash through you—they are the rain that clears your sky.

Affirmation

"I honor my emotions as sacred teachers. Each release brings renewal."

Breath Ritual

Inhale: "I allow."Exhale: "I release."
Repeat until your body softens like earth after rain.

Dream Summary

You walk through a thunderstorm. Rain soaks you completely, but when it clears, the world feels pure and alive.

Symbolic Meaning

Storm: Emotional release and necessary cleansing.

Rain: Renewal and emotional healing.

After the Storm: Peace through acceptance.

Dream Log

Track your dreams, symbols, and insights

Journal Prompts

What emotions have I been avoiding that need release?
How can I allow myself to feel without judgment?
What comes after my personal storms?

The Shedding Snake - Transformation and Renewal

You are shedding the old layers that no longer fit your truth. Honor your evolution and trust your body's wisdom.

Affirmation

"I release the past with gratitude. My renewal brings power and clarity."

Breath Ritual

Take a deep breath and imagine exhaling an old layer of self. Inhale new light into the space created.

Symbolic Meaning

Snake: Healing, renewal, rebirth through change.

Shedding Skin: Letting go of outdated beliefs or roles.

Transformation: Embracing personal evolution and power.

Dream Summary

You witness a snake slowly shedding its old skin. Beneath it gleams a vibrant new pattern—alive, renewed, whole.

Dream Log

Emotion, Message, Insight for each dream

Journal Prompts

What beliefs or habits am I ready to release?
How can I embrace my next chapter with confidence?
What wisdom is revealed when I let go of the old?

The Blossoming Garden – Clarity That Cuts Through Illusion

Your efforts are blooming into beauty. Growth takes time, but every seed of intention blossoms in divine timing.

Affirmation

"I blossom with grace. My growth is unfolding in perfect time."

Breath Ritual

Breathe in the scent of imaginary blossoms.
Exhale gratitude for your personal garden of life.

Dream Summary

You walk through a lush garden filled with vibrant blooms. Each flower seems to open as you pass by, releasing gentle fragrance and light.

Symbolic Meaning

Garden: Growth, nurturing, patience, creation.

Blooming Flowers: The fruition of inner work.

Fragrance: Gratitude and joy in the process of becoming.

Dream Log

Emotion, Message, Insight for each dream

Journal Prompts

What have I been nurturing that's beginning to bloom?
How can I cultivate patience and trust during growth?
How can I celebrate progress even before full results appear?

The Sword of Truth – Clarity That Cuts Through Illusion

Truth is your power. When you speak and act with integrity, confusion dissolves and strength rises.

Affirmation

"My truth is my strength. I wield clarity with grace and courage."

Symbolic Meaning

Sword: Clarity, truth, and cutting through illusion.

Raising It: Empowerment, confidence, readiness to face challenges.

Clearing Fog: Gaining perspective and discernment.

Breath Ritual

Breath Ritual:
Inhale: "Truth."
Exhale: "Power."
Visualize a line of light running from your heart to your throat, clearing your voice.

Dream Summary

You hold a shining sword that hums with energy. When you raise it, the fog clears around you, and everything becomes sharp and defined.

Dream Log

Emotion, Message, Insight for each dream

Journal Prompts

Where do I need to speak or stand in my truth?
What illusions or doubts am I ready to cut away?
How can I use clarity as a tool for peace, not battle?

The Inner Warrior – Strength in Spirit and Purpose

True strength is calm and grounded. You are not fighting life —you are leading with purpose and focus.

Affirmation

"I am a peaceful warrior. My strength comes from inner balance."

Breath Ritual

Stand tall. Inhale through your nose for 4 counts, exhale for 6. Feel your feet grounded and your energy centered in your core.

Dream Summary

You see yourself as a warrior in calm readiness—not in battle, but in sacred stillness before action. Strength radiates from within.

Symbolic Meaning

Warrior: Discipline, courage, resilience, and purpose.

Stillness Before Battle: Mastery through self-control.

Armor: Boundaries that protect without closing off love.

Dream Log

Emotion, Message, Insight for each dream

Journal Prompts

What does being a warrior of peace mean to me?
Where can I show courage through calmness instead of
conflict?
How do I honor my power without aggression?

The Volcano's Fire – Power of Release and Creation

Suppressed power eventually demands expression. Channel passion consciously—your intensity can become creation instead of chaos.

Affirmation

"My fire transforms me. I express passion with purpose and wisdom."

Symbolic Meaning

Volcano: Repressed energy or emotion ready for release.

Eruption: Expression, catharsis, transformation through intensity.

Lava Light: Purification and new creation from destruction.

Breath Ritual

Inhale through the nose, visualize a warm glow in your belly. Exhale slowly through the mouth, releasing pressure and softening.

Dream Summary

You stand near a dormant volcano that begins to rumble. Instead of fear, you feel awe—the eruption releases brilliant molten light into the sky.

Dream Log

Emotion, Message, Insight for each dream

Journal Prompts

What feelings or truths am I holding back?
How can I release strong emotions in healthy ways?
What beauty or renewal can rise from my intensity?

The Mountaintop Victory – Triumph of Spirit and Vision

You've earned your strength through effort. Celebrate progress and rest in the awareness of how far you've come.

Affirmation

"I honor my journey. Each step has shaped my strength and vision."

Breath Ritual

Inhale fresh air through the nose. Exhale relief and pride. Visualize standing on a mountaintop of light.

Dream Summary

After a long climb, you reach the summit of a high mountain. The view expands infinitely, and you feel light, powerful, and free.

Symbolic Meaning

Mountaintop: Achievement, mastery, higher awareness.

Climb: The journey through perseverance and courage.

View from Above: Perspective gained through discipline.

Dream Log

Emotion, Message, Insight for each dream

Journal Prompts

What challenge have I conquered recently?
How can I celebrate small victories more often?
What new goals lie beyond this summit?

The Voice of Power – Expression of Authentic Truth

Your voice carries energy that shapes worlds. Speak with intention and allow authenticity to lead your expression.

Affirmation

"My voice is powerful and pure. I express myself with courage and clarity."

Symbolic Meaning

Voice: Expression of truth and authenticity.

Sound or Song: Alignment between heart and action.

Vibration: The creative force of words and intention.

Breath Ritual

Take a deep breath into your throat center. On your exhale, hum softly, feeling vibration release tension and open your expression.

Dream Summary

You open your mouth to speak or sing, and a powerful sound emerges—resonant and beautiful. The vibration fills the space with light.

Dream Log

Emotion, Message, Insight for each dream

Journal Prompts

Where do I need to speak my truth with more confidence?
How can I use my voice for healing or inspiration?
What message am I here to share?

The Blooming Lotus – Enlightenment Rising from the Depths

You have become the embodiment of your journey—rooted in the mud, yet blooming in grace. Your light now rises naturally to bless the world.

Affirmation

"I am the lotus of divine truth. My presence radiates love and peace."

Breath Ritual

Inhale deeply through your crown. Exhale gently through your heart. Visualize a lotus unfurling with each breath.

Dream Summary

You see a lotus flower rise from calm water. Its petals open slowly, revealing radiant light within. The reflection shimmers, uniting heaven and earth.

Symbolic Meaning

Lotus: Enlightenment, purity, awakening through experience.

Water: Emotional wisdom and the sacred feminine.

Light Within: Illumination of the divine self.

Dream Log

Emotion, Message, Insight for each dream

Journal Prompts

What qualities of my true nature am I ready to express more fully?
How have I grown through challenge into wisdom?
What does it mean to bloom from within?

The Body of Light – Radiance of Spirit Embodied

You are merging the human and the divine within. Every step you take in awareness emanates healing and harmony.

Affirmation

"I am a vessel of divine light. My presence uplifts and illuminates."

Symbolic Meaning

Light Body: Integration of spirit and form.

Glow: Enlightened awareness and peaceful energy.

Movement: Living your divine truth in action.

Breath Ritual

Breathe in through your crown; imagine light flooding every cell.
Exhale serenity through your entire being.

Dream Summary

In your dream, your body glows with soft golden light. You move effortlessly, weightless, surrounded by gentle radiance.

Dream Log

Emotion, Message, Insight for each dream

Journal Prompts

How can I honor my body as a vessel of light?
What daily rituals help me stay connected to my higher self?
Where in my life do I naturally radiate peace?

The Sacred Dance – Union of Movement and Spirit

Life is a dance of spirit in motion. When you release control and move from the heart, you embody divine harmony.

Affirmation

"I am the dance of creation. Joy moves through me in perfect rhythm."

Breath Ritual

Inhale: "Flow." Exhale: "Grace."
Sway gently with each breath until you feel attuned to life's rhythm.

Dream Summary

You find yourself dancing in a circle of golden light. Each movement feels guided by grace and joy, as if the universe is moving through you.

Symbolic Meaning

Dance: Joy, embodiment, sacred flow.

Circle of Light: Wholeness and unity.

Movement: Surrender to divine rhythm.

Dream Log

Emotion, Message, Insight for each dream

Journal Prompts

Where do I feel most free and alive?
How can I let joy guide my choices?
What happens when I move without fear of judgment?

The Guiding Stars – Direction from the Celestial Realms

You are divinely guided. Even in darkness, your path shines with purpose—trust the celestial rhythm of your becoming.

Affirmation

"The light of the cosmos lives in my heart. I walk guided by divine wisdom."

Symbolic Meaning

Stars: Divine guidance, destiny, cosmic truth.

Light Anchoring to Heart: Connection between infinite and personal.

Night Sky: Peaceful trust in the unseen.

Breath Ritual

Look upward with soft eyes. Inhale starlight into your heart. Exhale love back into the universe.

Dream Summary

You stand under a vast night sky filled with brilliant stars. One star pulses brighter, and you feel its light anchor into your heart.

Dream Log

Emotion, Message, Insight for each dream

Journal Prompts

What "stars" (signs, people, or dreams) are guiding me right now?
How can I deepen my faith in unseen guidance?
When do I feel most connected to the infinite?

The White Animal Messenger – Purity of Guidance and Instinct

You are walking in grace. Purity of heart opens channels of guidance—listen, and the sacred will speak.

Affirmation

"I walk in divine peace. My heart is open, my spirit is light."

Breath Ritual

Breathe softly through the nose. On each exhale, whisper gratitude. Feel peace ripple outward from your heart.

Dream Summary

A white deer approaches you in stillness, or a dove lands softly on your hand. The moment feels sacred, like a quiet blessing.

Symbolic Meaning

White Animals: Purity, peace, and spiritual mastery.

Messenger: Communication from higher consciousness.

Calm Presence: Harmony with the natural and divine worlds.

Dream Log

Emotion, Message, Insight for each dream

Journal Prompts

What gentle signs of guidance have appeared lately?
How can I walk through life with more reverence and peace?
What blessings am I ready to acknowledge?

The Flight —
Freedom and Fear

"Rise beyond fear. You were born to experience life from higher vision."

Affirmation

"I am both grounded and free."

Breath Ritual

Inhale deeply through the heart, feeling air fill your chest like wings expanding.
Exhale gently, releasing weight from your shoulders.
Whisper: "I am light; I am lifted."

Dream Summary

You soar, hover, or struggle to lift off — feeling exhilaration, fear, or wonder.

Symbolic Meaning

Flight represents liberation and perspective — transcending limitations.
If fear arises, it reflects uncertainty about success or freedom.
This dream invites you to trust your wings and redefine what safety means.

Dream Log

Emotion, Message, Insight for each dream

Journal Prompts

Where am I ready to expand beyond limits?
What fear keeps me tethered when I could fly?
How can I balance freedom with grounding?

The House — The Inner Self

"You are exploring the architecture of your soul. Every room, even the dusty ones, deserves light."

Affirmation

"I welcome light into every room of my being."

Symbolic Meaning

The House is your inner world. Each room mirrors a part of your psyche: the kitchen for nourishment, the bedroom for intimacy, the attic for memories, the basement for the subconscious.

Breath Ritual

Inhale deeply, visualizing golden light flowing through each "room" of your body.
Exhale gently, releasing any clutter or heaviness.
Whisper: "I am home within myself."

Dream Summary

You wander through a house — perhaps familiar, perhaps strange — exploring rooms or hidden spaces.

Dream Log

Emotion, Message, Insight for each dream

Journal Prompts

What room or area stood out in my dream?
What part of my inner life is asking for attention or care?
How can I make my inner home feel more like sanctuary?

The Car —
Direction and Control

"Take the wheel of your own journey. You are capable of guiding your life with awareness and trust."

Affirmation

"I steer my journey with mindful confidence."

Breath Ritual

Inhale deeply, envisioning a clear open road.
Exhale slowly, releasing pressure to rush.
Whisper: "I drive with ease."

Dream Summary

You drive, coast, or find yourself a passenger in a car.
The road may be smooth, winding, or uncertain.

Symbolic Meaning

The Car represents movement, life direction, and personal control.
Who drives and how you feel shows your relationship with momentum and decision-making.

Dream Log

Emotion, Message, Insight for each dream

Journal Prompts

Who was driving, and how did it make me feel?
Where in life am I steering versus being carried?
How can I slow down and still feel purposeful?

The Child — Renewal and Innocence

"Reclaim your wonder. Let play, curiosity, and simplicity be your teachers again."

Affirmation

"I nurture the child within with love and patience."

Symbolic Meaning

The Child symbolizes innocence, curiosity, and new beginnings.

It reminds you of your innate joy and creativity.

To dream of a child is to be invited to protect and nurture your inner light.

Breath Ritual

Place a hand on your heart and one on your belly.
Inhale deeply, feeling warmth spread between both.
Exhale softly, smiling: "I am safe to be new again."

Dream Summary

A child appears — laughing, crying, or reaching for you. Sometimes it's your younger self.

Dream Log

Emotion, Message, Insight for each dream

Journal Prompts

What part of my innocence wants to return?
How can I bring more play into my daily life?
What new chapter is asking for my nurturing attention?

The Cat – Intuition and Independence

"Move softly and trust the unseen. You already know the truth — your intuition is the lamp lighting the path ahead."
The cat teaches that power need not roar; sometimes the quietest knowing is the truest strength.

Affirmation

"I honor my intuition and move through life with quiet confidence."

Breath Ritual

Sit comfortably and close your eyes.
Inhale slowly through the nose, feeling your spine lengthen — steady and poised.
Hold for a moment, listening to the silence behind the breath.
Exhale softly through the mouth, whispering:
"I trust my inner knowing."
Repeat three times, imagining a soft, golden cat's-eye light glowing in your heart — the flame of instinct and calm awareness.

Dream Summary

A cat appears — sleek, silent, perhaps brushing against you or watching with curious eyes. It may ignore your call or curl softly into your presence. The dream feels familiar, like meeting an old friend whose language is intuition itself.

Symbolic Meaning

The cat is a guardian of intuition and mystery. Moving between worlds with quiet grace, it embodies sovereignty, discernment, and inner knowing.

When cats visit in dreams, they often reflect your relationship with trusting yourself — reminding you that instinct is sacred, and independence can coexist with deep connection.

A cat's presence may signal that it's time to rely less on external approval and more on your own guidance. If the cat is injured, hiding, or ignored, it suggests intuition you've neglected or doubted.

Dream Log

Emotion, Message, Insight for each dream

Journal Prompts

Where in my life am I being guided to follow my intuition instead of reason?
How do I honor my independence without closing myself off?
What boundary is asking to be strengthened or redefined right now?

Pregnancy — Creation and Becoming

"Something beautiful is forming in divine timing. Protect your process, nurture it with faith, and allow it to grow unseen until it is ready to shine."

Affirmation

"I am fertile with possibility. I trust the rhythm of divine creation."

Symbolic Meaning

Pregnancy dreams reveal potential and creativity gestating within. They do not always point to physical birth, but to the emergence of ideas, projects, or emotional growth.

These dreams remind you that creation happens in stillness before visibility.

Breath Ritual

Place both hands over your lower belly.
Inhale through your nose, imagining light gathering there.
Exhale softly through your mouth, whispering: "I nurture what grows in me."

Dream Summary

You dream of carrying new life — a child, an egg, a swelling belly — or simply the awareness of something forming inside you. The feeling is both tender and sacred.

Dream Log

Emotion, Message, Insight for each dream

Journal Prompts

What new idea or identity is quietly growing within me?

How can I protect my creative or emotional process from premature exposure?

Where am I being asked to wait and trust rather than rush?

Death of Self — Transformation and Renewal

"A chapter of your identity is complete. The death you feel is liberation — the making of space for a truer you to emerge."

Affirmation

"I release who I was with love and awaken to who I am becoming."

Breath Ritual

Inhale deeply through the heart, visualizing white light filling your chest.
Hold briefly — acknowledge what is ending.
Exhale through the mouth, whispering: "I am free to begin again."

Dream Summary

You witness your own passing, watch yourself fade, or feel a release of life within the dream. Fear may arise — yet peace often follows.

Symbolic Meaning

This dream rarely predicts physical death; instead, it symbolizes rebirth. An old self, pattern, or belief has fulfilled its role. The psyche dramatizes its release through the metaphor of death so you can consciously welcome renewal.

Dream Log

Emotion, Message, Insight for each dream

Journal Prompts

What part of me feels ready to end or transform?
What am I releasing with love and gratitude rather than resistance?
What new energy or identity is being born within me?

The Moon — Intuition and Mystery

"Trust the unseen phases of your becoming. What is hidden will wax again in its own divine time."

Affirmation

"I move in harmony with the rhythm of the Moon within me."

Breath Ritual

Inhale deeply, imagining moonlight entering your crown.
Hold for a gentle heartbeat.
Exhale slowly, whispering: "I trust my inner tides."

Symbolic Meaning

The Moon governs tides, dreams, and intuition.
She waxes and wanes, reminding you that energy, emotion, and creativity move in cycles.
To dream of her is to reconnect with your inner rhythm and sacred feminine knowing.

Dream Summary

You see or feel the Moon — full and radiant, eclipsed or new.
It calls your gaze upward, stirring emotion or awe.

Dream Log

Emotion, Message, Insight for each dream

Journal Prompts

Which phase of life am I currently in — new, full, or releasing?
How do I honor my intuition when logic resists?
What area of my life feels ready to illuminate?

Death of a Parent — Ancestral Healing and Maturity

"You are stepping into your own authority. Bless what your parents gave, forgive what they could not, and continue the lineage in light."

Affirmation

"I honor my lineage and carry forward only what is love."

Symbolic Meaning

The death of a parent in dreams marks an inner rite of passage. It signals the end of reliance on external authority and the rise of self-leadership. This dream can also bring ancestral healing — releasing generational pain so you can live freely in your own truth.

Breath Ritual

Inhale through the nose, imagining light moving through your roots — ancestors behind you, guiding. Exhale gently, sending gratitude through your heart to them. Whisper softly: "I bless the past and walk free."

Dream Summary

A parent passes or departs in the dream. You may feel sadness, calm, or profound knowing — the sensation that something sacred has completed.

Dream Log

Emotion, Message, Insight for each dream

Journal Prompts

What wisdom or wound from my lineage is ready to transform?

How can I honor my parents' legacy while living my own purpose?

What freedom arises when I stand as the elder of my own path?

Lunar Cycle Dream Tracker

Moon Phases

Track your dreams and intentions throughout the lunar cycle.

New Moon Reflections

Reflection Questions for Personal Growth

The **New Moon phase** symbolizes a fresh start and an invitation to reflect on your innermost desires. Take a moment to connect with your thoughts and emotions, allowing them to surface as you respond to the following questions. This is a sacred time for setting intentions and embracing the opportunities that await you on your journey.

Full Moon Reflection

Reflection

Engage in **sacred introspection** during this lunar phase.

Under the full moon, revisit your dreams and notice recurring symbols.

Which dream themes showed up this month?

What does my subconscious want me to embrace?

Where have I grown in feeling secure and supported?

Full Moon Affirmation
"I celebrate my progress. I stand firmly in love, guided by trust and intuition."

Moonlight Ritual for Dream Recall

Before bed, sit near a window or candle flame.
Breathe in the night's quiet. Whisper your invitation:

Affirmation

"I am ready to remember."

Tonight's intention:

Symbol or phrase that feels alive:

Salt Bath for Clearing

Mix sea salt, a few drops of lavender or cedar oil, and a prayer.

As the water swirls, say:

"I release the day and return to peace."
 Soak until thoughts dissolve.

What I'm releasing tonight:

What peace feels like in my body:

Morning Integration Meditation

On waking, close your eyes before reaching for anything.

Ask: "What stayed with me from my dream?"
Visualize it as a symbol glowing in your chest.
Breathe it into gratitude.

Symbol remembered:

Lesson or feeling carried forward:

Dream Crystals

Amethyst – spiritual clarity
Celestite – gentle dream messages
Labradorite – protection in sleep

Place one near your pillow, cleanse weekly in moonlight.

Which crystal calls to me this week?

Herbal Allies for Rest

Infuse your night with herbs that soothe the nervous system and invite sacred sleep.

Lavender: peace
Mugwort: lucid dreaming
Chamomile: comfort
Lemon balm: gentle calm

Tonight's blend or tea ritual:

Dream Jar Ritual

Write your bedtime intention on paper.
Fold it, place in a jar with a sprinkle of salt or herbs.
Each morning, read and note what surfaced.
Empty and refresh at the New Moon.

This cycle's dream focus:

Dream Log

Emotion, Message, Insight for each dream

Journal Prompts

What emotion visits me most often in my dreams
lately, and what might it need me to acknowledge?
If my subconscious wrote me a love letter, what would
it say?
How do my dreams mirror my current
transformations?
What symbols follow me from one dream to another?
What would it look like to live the wisdom of one
recent dream?

Sacred Sleep & Gratitude

Night Prayer for the Dreamer

"May my sleep be sanctuary.
 May my dreams speak truth in symbols of light.
 May I awaken renewed, remembering I am guided."

Evening Gratitude:

One thing I release tonight: _____
One thing I welcome: _____
One blessing from today: _____

Affirmations for Rest

"I am safe to surrender to rest."
"My body renews as my spirit journeys."
"Dreams bring me insight in perfect measure."

Dream Log

Emotion, Message, Insight for each dream

Nightly Intention Page

Journal beside bed
Candle or oil lit
Phone silenced
Breath softened
Affirmation spoken

Tonight's Intention: _____

Symbol I invite: _____

Dream Log

Emotion, Message, Insight for each dream

Final Blessing

A Heartfelt Message for You

As you close this journal, may the **light of your dreams** illuminate your path. Embrace the journey of self-discovery and trust in the unfolding of your intuition.

This journal is your sacred companion, guiding you toward **transformation** and divine awakening. Remember, you carry the essence of joy within you—nurture it and let it flourish.

The Return to Light

When the last page has been filled and the final moon has waned,
know this—your journey has only just begun.

Every dream recorded, every reflection written, has shaped a deeper
harmony
between your waking life and your eternal soul.

You have walked through shadow and radiance.

You have conversed with stars, with symbols, with silence.

You have remembered yourself as both the question and the answer,
the seed and the bloom, the dream and the dreamer.

"The light you sought was never lost—it was waiting for your eyes to open."

May the peace of knowing rest within you.
May love move through your words, your choices, your creations.
And may you continue to walk as one who remembers that life itself is the
most luminous dream of all.

Author's Note

A Journey of Spiritual Awakening and Reflection

As you explore this journal, may it serve as a **gentle companion** in your journey of self-discovery.

Embrace each page as an opportunity for connection, reflection, and growth. Your dreams and intuitions hold profound insights waiting to unfold.

Trust in this sacred process and allow your spirit to soar.

At TrueJoy Living, we believe transformation is sacred, cyclical, and deeply personal.

This journal was created as a devotional companion to your awakening—a bridge between the inner world of dreams and the outer world of purpose.

Whether you began with curiosity, healing, or longing, know that your journey here is holy.

Author's Note

A Journey of Spiritual Awakening and Reflection

You have communed with your subconscious and your soul,
gathered wisdom from
the unseen, and awakened the quiet voice of divine
remembrance.

*"May your nights continue to whisper wisdom,
And may your days unfold as living prayers of joy."*

With love from the sanctuary of TrueJoy Living—

For all who dream, awaken, and live in the light.

www.truejoy-living.com
@truejoy.living

Gratitude and Reflection

Thank you for embarking on this journey with your journal

We hope this journal serves as a **sacred tool** for your exploration of dreams and intuition. May it inspire deeper connections and **transformative experiences** as you navigate your spiritual path. Remember, each entry is a step towards enlightenment and understanding.

www.ingramcontent.com/pod-product-compliance
Lightning Source LLC
Chambersburg PA
CBHW041731140626
46547CB00026BA/451